Christmas Classics for Harmonica

25 Timeless Melodies for Easy Harmonica

Arranged by Eric J. Plahna

ISBN 978-1-4234-0448-4

7777 W. BLUEMOUND RD. P.O. BOX 13819 MILWAUKEE, WI 53213

In Australia Contact:
Hal Leonard Australia Pty. Ltd.
4 Lentara Court
Cheltenham, Victoria, 3192 Australia
Email: ausadmin@halleonard.com

Visit Hal Leonard Online at
www.halleonard.com

CONTENTS

INTRODUCTION

Welcome to *Christmas Classics for Harmonica*, a collection of 25 holiday songs arranged for easy harmonica. If you're a beginning harmonica player, you've come to the right place; these well-known songs will have you playing and enjoying music in no time! Each melody is presented in an easy-to-read format—including lyrics to help you follow along and chords for optional accompaniment. The harmonica tablature used in this book and discussed on the next page makes playing these Christmas Classics possible for anyone, even if you don't know how to read music.

As you play through the songs, feel free to choose your own tempo (speed); you can always speed up or slow down according to your ability and preference. Also, try playing some of the melodies with 2 or 3 holes at the same time instead of just one. You'll find that some of the songs sound better this way, while others are more suited to the one-hole approach, or even a mixture of the two.

First, the recommended way to hold your harmonica:

1. Make a "C" with your left hand.
2. Insert the harmonica as shown, holding it firmly but comfortably.
3. Keep your fingers arched slightly. This will allow you to control the sound better.

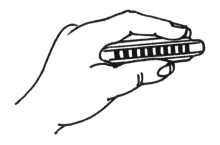

Your right hand should cup, or cradle, your left hand with the fingers coming up around your left hand pinky to form a seal.

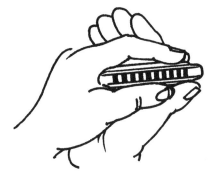

Ultimately of course, you get to choose the most comfortable way to play your harmonica.

HOW TO READ HARMONICA TABLATURE
or
YOU DON'T HAVE TO READ MUSIC TO PLAY THIS BOOK

10-Hole C Diatonic Harmonica

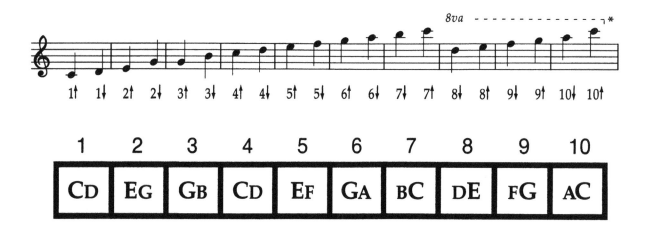

THE BASICS

1. For each note ♩, you are given the number of the hole you are to play.

2. An arrow pointing up ↑ to the right of the number means to **blow** (exhale) that note.

3. An arrow pointing down ↓ to the right of the number means to **draw** (inhale) that note.

Sounds one octave (8 notes) higher than written.

SINGLE NOTES

Single notes can be played in two different ways:

Tongue Blocking

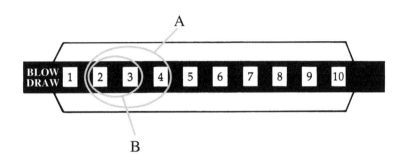

A. Cover three or four notes with your lips, *and...*
B. Cover all the holes with your tongue except the hole on the right

or…

Lipping

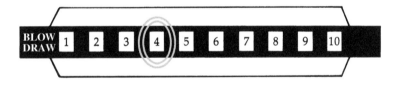

1. Pucker your lips so that air passes through one hole.
2. Relax the inside of your mouth, as if you were saying "ah" (very important for good tone).

Again, you may devise a way that is more comfortable for you to achieve a clean single-note sound. There are people who curl their tongue and isolate one tone hole that way.

Angels from the Realms of Glory

Words by James Montgomery
Music by Henry T. Smart

*Song sounds one octave higher than written.

Angels We Have Heard on High

Traditional French Carol
Translated by James Chadwick

As with Gladness Men of Old

Words by William Chatterton Dix
Music by Conrad Kocher

*Song sounds one octave higher than written.

Away in a Manger

Traditional
Music by William J. Kirkpatrick

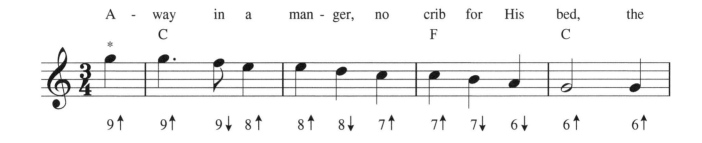

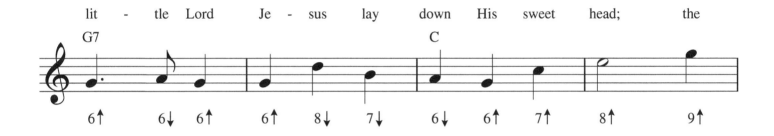

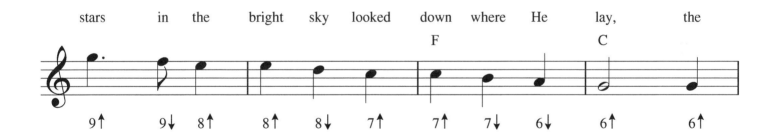

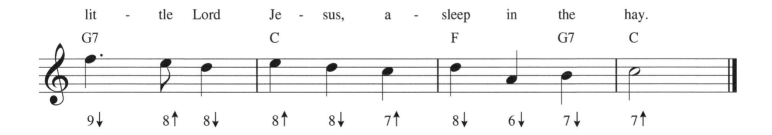

*Song sounds one octave higher than written.

Deck the Hall

Traditional Welsh Carol

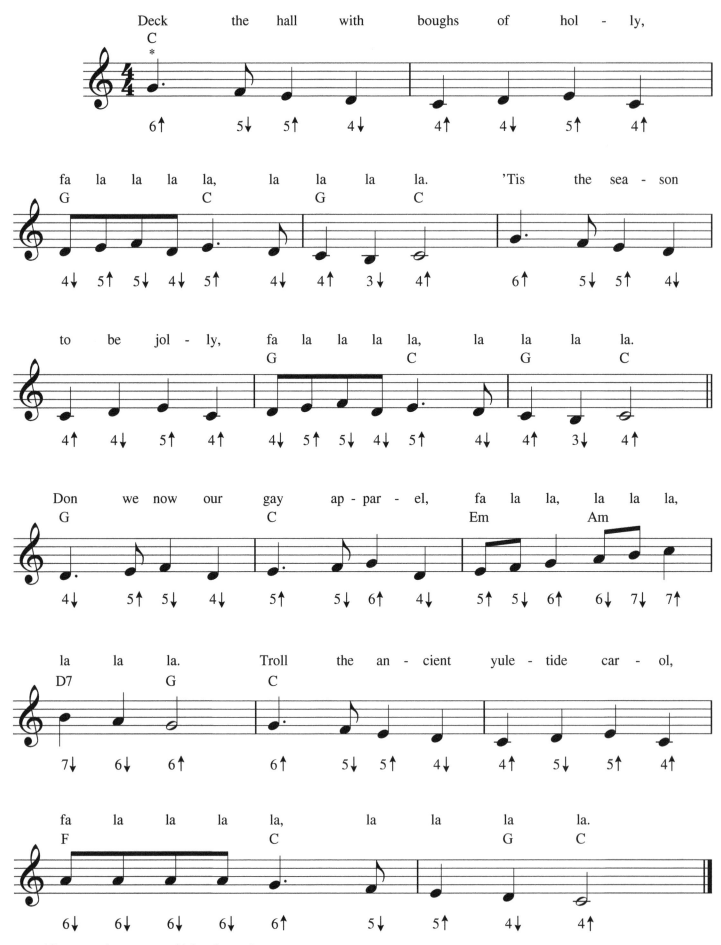

*Song sounds one octave higher than written.

Ding Dong! Merrily on High!

French Carol

*Song sounds one octave higher than written.

The First Noël

17th Century English Carol
Music from W. Sandy's Christmas Carols

*Song sounds one octave higher than written.

God Rest Ye Merry, Gentlemen

19th Century English Carol

*Song sounds one octave higher than written.

Good Christian Men, Rejoice

14th Century Latin Text
Translated by John Mason Neale
14th Century German Melody

*Song sounds one octave higher than written.

Good King Wenceslas

Words by John M. Neale
Music from Piae Cantiones

*Song sounds one octave higher than written.

Hark! The Herald Angels Sing

Words by Charles Wesley
Altered by George Whitefield
Music by Felix Mendelssohn-Bartholdy
Arranged by William H. Cummings

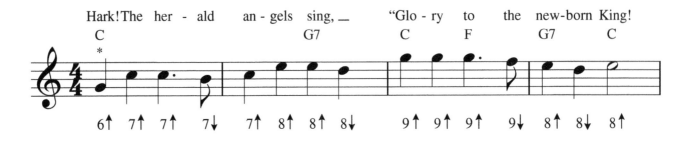

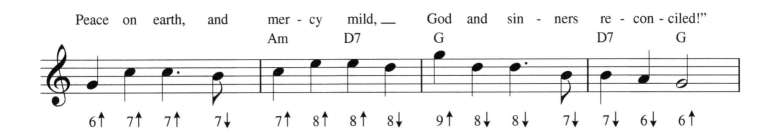

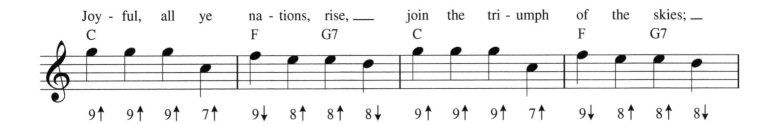

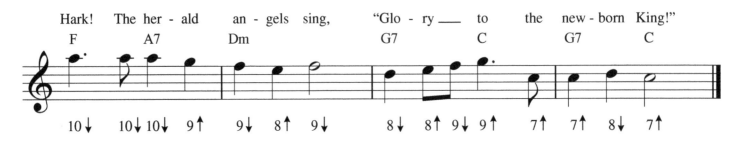

*Song sounds one octave higher than written.

The Holly and the Ivy

18th Century English Carol

*Song sounds one octave higher than written.

I Saw Three Ships

Traditional English Carol

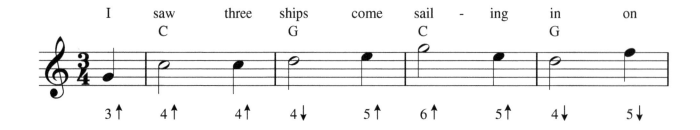

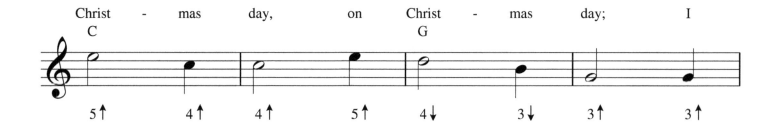

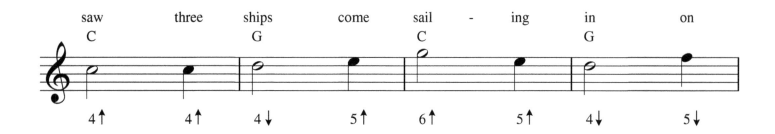

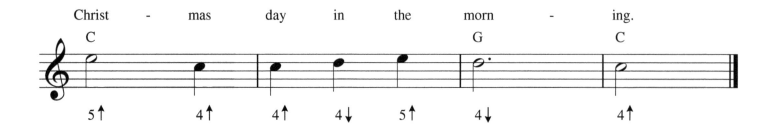

Jolly Old Saint Nicholas

Traditional 19th Century American Carol

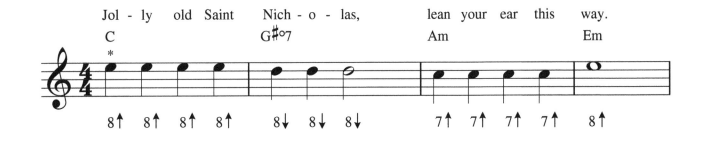

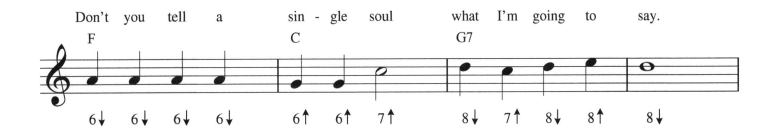

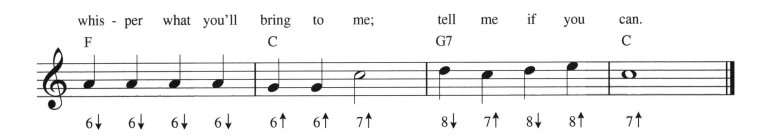

*Song sounds one octave higher than written.

Jingle Bells

Words and Music by J. Pierpont

*Verse sounds one octave higher than written.

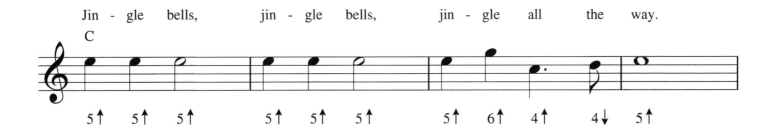

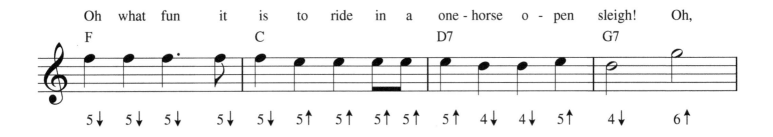

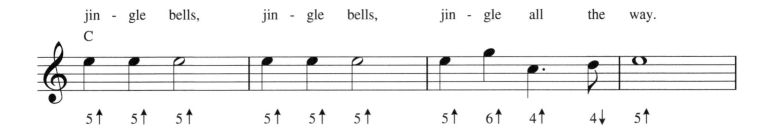

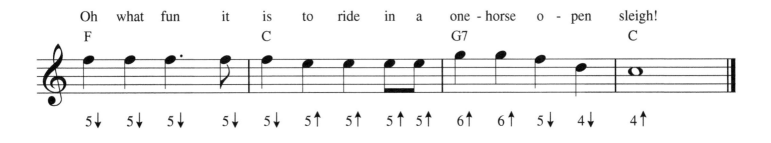

Joy to the World

Words by Isaac Watts
Music by George Frideric Handel
Arranged by Lowell Mason

*Song sounds one octave higher than written.

O Come, All Ye Faithful

(Adeste Fideles)

Words and Music by John Francis Wade
Latin Words translated by Frederick Oakeley

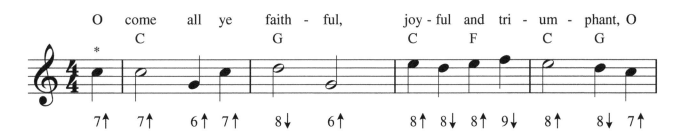

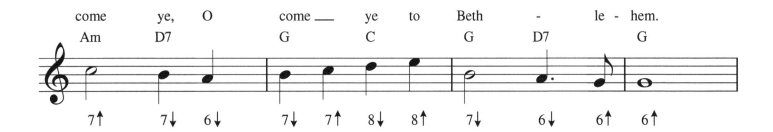

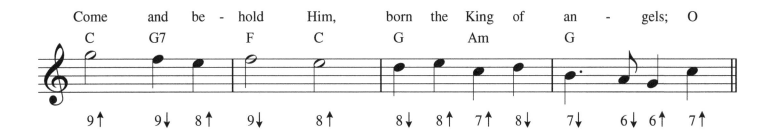

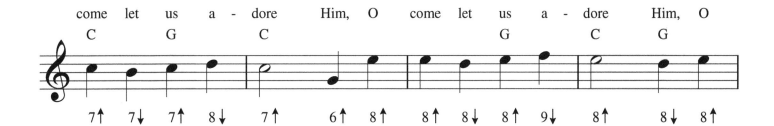

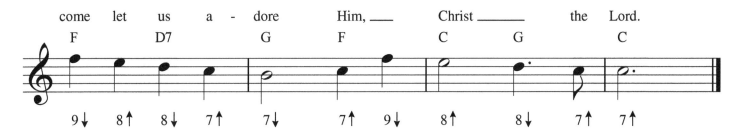

*Song sounds one octave higher than written.

O Holy Night

French Words by Placide Cappeau
English Words by John S. Dwight
Music by Adolphe Adam

O ho - ly night ___ the stars are bright - ly shin - ing, it is the

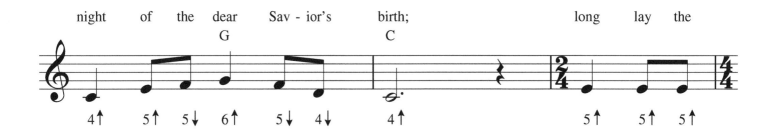

night of the dear Sav - ior's birth; long lay the

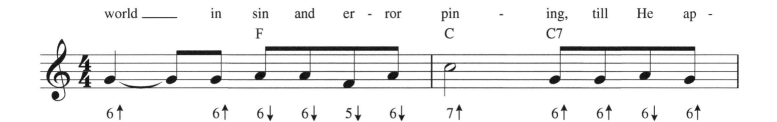

world ___ in sin and er - ror pin - ing, till He ap -

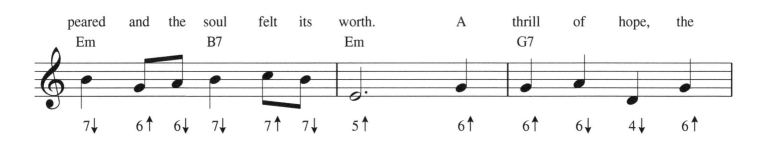

peared and the soul felt its worth. A thrill of hope, the

*Song sounds one octave higher than written.

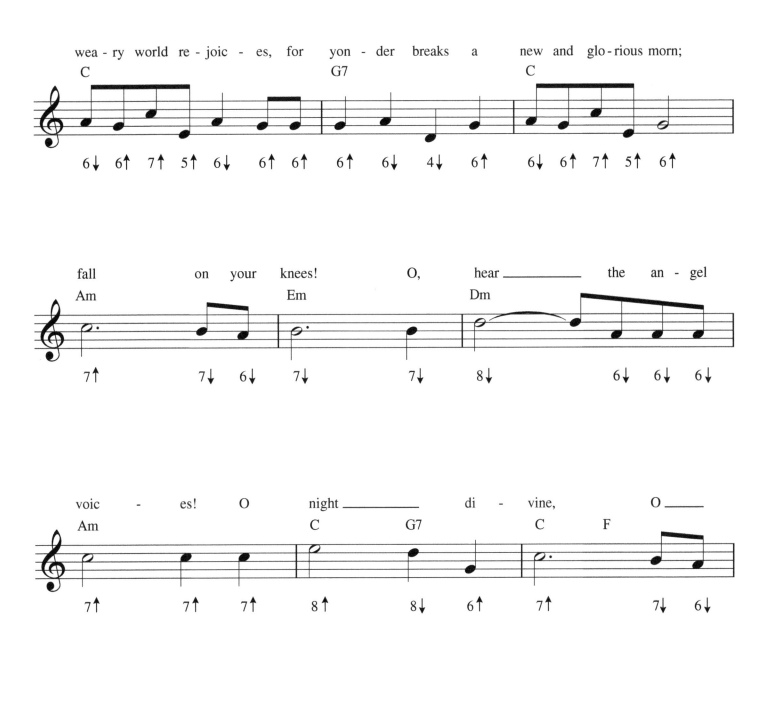

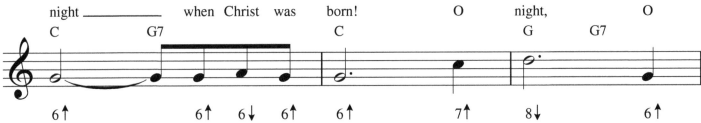

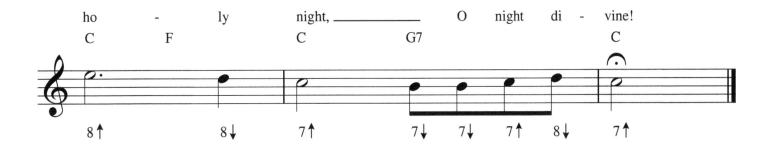

O Come, O Come, Emmanuel

Traditional Latin Text
Translated by John M. Neale
15th Century French Melody
Adapted by Thomas Helmore

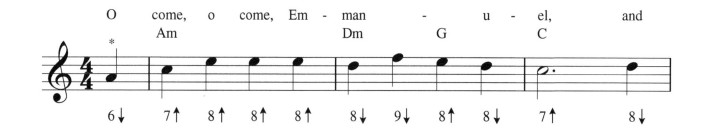

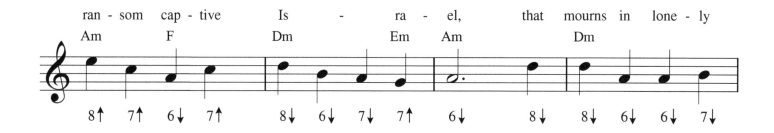

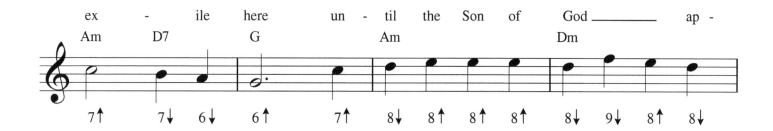

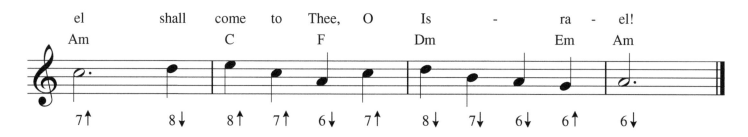

*Song sounds one octave higher than written.

O Tannenbaum
(O Christmas Tree)
Traditional German Carol

Silent Night

Words by Joseph Mohr
Translated by John F. Young
Music by Franz X. Gruber

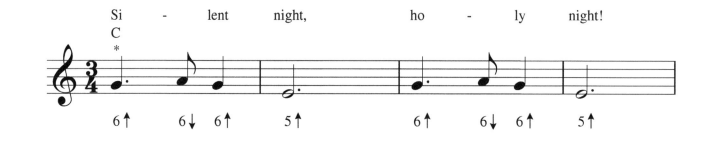

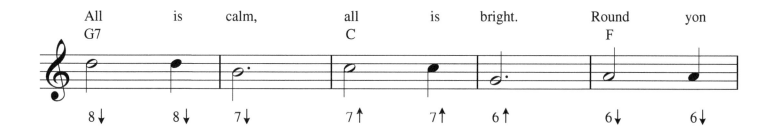

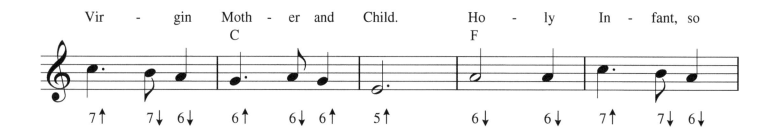

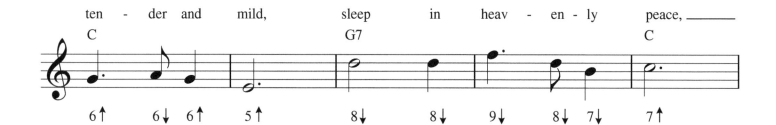

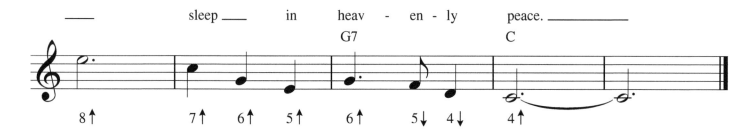

*Song sounds one octave higher than written.

Up on the Housetop

Words and Music by B.R. Handy

*Song sounds one octave higher than written.

We Three Kings of Orient Are

Words and Music by John H. Hopkins, Jr.

*Song sounds one octave higher than written.

We Wish You a Merry Christmas

Traditional English Folksong

*Song sounds one octave higher than written.

While Shepherds Watched Their Flocks

Words by Nahum Tate
Music by George Frideric Handel

*Song sounds one octave higher than written.

THE HAL LEONARD HARMONICA METHOD AND SONGBOOKS

THE METHOD

THE HAL LEONARD COMPLETE HARMONICA METHOD — CHROMATIC HARMONICA
by Bobby Joe Holman

The only harmonica method to present the chromatic harmonica in 14 scales and modes in all 12 keys! This book will take beginners from the basics on through to the most advanced techniques available for the contemporary harmonica player. Each section contains appropriate songs and exercises that enable the player to quickly learn the various concepts presented. Every aspect of this versatile musical instrument is explored and explained in easy-to-understand detail with illustrations. The musical styles covered include traditional, blues, pop and rock.

00841286 Book/Online Audio............................ $12.99

THE HAL LEONARD COMPLETE HARMONICA METHOD — DIATONIC HARMONICA
by Bobby Joe Holman

The only harmonica method specific to the diatonic harmonica, covering all six positions. This book/audio pack contains over 20 songs and musical examples that take beginners from the basics on through to the most advanced techniques available for the contemporary harmonica player. Each section contains appropriate songs and exercises (which are demonstrated through the online video) that enable the player to quickly learn the various concepts presented. Every aspect of this versatile musical instrument is explored and explained in easy-to-understand detail with illustrations. The musical styles covered include traditional, blues, pop and rock.

00841285 Book/Online Audio............................ $12.99

THE SONGBOOKS

The Hal Leonard Harmonica Songbook series offers a wide variety of music especially tailored to the two-volume Hal Leonard Harmonica Method, but can be played by all harmonica players, diatonic and chromatic alike. All books include study and performance notes, and a guide to harmonica tablature. From classical themes to Christmas music, rock and roll to Broadway, there's something for everyone!

BROADWAY SONGS FOR HARMONICA **INCLUDES TAB**
arranged by Bobby Joe Holman

19 show-stopping Broadway tunes for the harmonica. Songs include: Ain't Misbehavin' • Bali Ha'i • Camelot • Climb Ev'ry Mountain • Do-Re-Mi • Edelweiss • Give My Regards to Broadway • Hello, Dolly! • I've Grown Accustomed to Her Face • The Impossible Dream (The Quest) • Memory • Oklahoma • People • and more.

00820009...$9.95

CLASSICAL FAVORITES FOR HARMONICA **INCLUDES TAB**
arranged by Bobby Joe Holman

18 famous classical melodies and themes, arranged for diatonic and chromatic players. Includes: By the Beautiful Blue Danube • Clair De Lune • The Flight of the Bumble Bee • Gypsy Rondo • Moonlight Sonata • Surprise Symphony • The Swan (Le Cygne) • Waltz of the Flowers • and more, plus a guide to harmonica tablature.

00820006...$10.99

MOVIE FAVORITES FOR HARMONICA **INCLUDES TAB**
arranged by Bobby Joe Holman

19 songs from the silver screen, arranged for diatonic and chromatic harmonica. Includes: Alfie • Bless the Beasts and Children • Chim Chim Cher-ee • The Entertainer • Georgy Girl • Midnight Cowboy • Moon River • Picnic • Speak Softly, Love • Stormy Weather • Tenderly • Unchained Melody • What a Wonderful World • and more, plus a guide to harmonica tablature.

00820014 ....$9.95

HAL•LEONARD®

CHRISTMAS COLLECTIONS
FROM HAL LEONARD
ALL BOOKS ARRANGED FOR PIANO, VOICE & GUITAR

The Best Christmas Songs Ever – 6th Edition
69 all-time favorites are included in the 6th edition of this collection of Christmas tunes. Includes: Auld Lang Syne • Coventry Carol • Frosty the Snow Man • Happy Holiday • It Came Upon the Midnight Clear • O Holy Night • Rudolph the Red-Nosed Reindeer • Silver Bells • What Child Is This? • and many more.
00359130...$27.50

The Big Book of Christmas Songs – 2nd Edition
An outstanding collection of over 120 all-time Christmas favorites and hard-to-find classics. Features: Angels We Have Heard on High • As Each Happy Christmas • Auld Lang Syne • The Boar's Head Carol • Christ Was Born on Christmas Day • Bring a Torch Jeannette, Isabella • Carol of the Bells • Coventry Carol • Deck the Halls • The First Noel • The Friendly Beasts • God Rest Ye Merry Gentlemen • I Heard the Bells on Christmas Day • It Came Upon a Midnight Clear • Jesu, Joy of Man's Desiring • Joy to the World • Masters in This Hall • O Holy Night • The Story of the Shepherd • 'Twas the Night Before Christmas • What Child Is This? • and many more. Includes guitar chord frames.
00311520...$19.95

Christmas Songs – Budget Books
Save some money this Christmas with this fabulous budget-priced collection of 100 holiday favorites: All I Want for Christmas Is You • Christmas Time Is Here • Feliz Navidad • Grandma Got Run Over by a Reindeer • Happy Holiday • I'll Be Home for Christmas • Jesus Born on This Day • Last Christmas • Merry Christmas, Baby • O Holy Night • Please Come Home for Christmas • Rockin' Around the Christmas Tree • Some Children See Him • We Need a Little Christmas • What Child Is This? • and more.
00310887...$14.99

The Definitive Christmas Collection – 3rd Edition
Revised with even more Christmas classics, this must-have 3rd edition contains 127 top songs, such as: Blue Christmas • Christmas Time Is Here • Do You Hear What I Hear • The First Noel • A Holly Jolly Christmas • Jingle-Bell Rock • Little Saint Nick • Merry Christmas, Darling • O Holy Night • Rudolph, the Red-Nosed Reindeer • Silver and Gold • We Need a Little Christmas • You're All I Want for Christmas • and more!
00311602...$24.95

The Most Requested Christmas Songs
This giant collection features nearly 70 holiday classics, from traditional carols to modern Christmas hits: Blue Christmas • Christmas Time Is Here • Deck the Hall • Feliz Navidad • I'll Be Home for Christmas • Jingle Bells • Little Saint Nick • Nuttin' for Christmas • Rudolph the Red-Nosed Reindeer • Silent Night • and more.
00001563...$19.99

The Muppet Christmas Carol
Matching folio to the blockbuster movie featuring 11 Muppet carols and eight pages of color photos. Bless Us All • Chairman of the Board • Christmas Scat • Finale - When Love Is Found/It Feels like Christmas • It Feels like Christmas • Marley and Marley • One More Sleep 'Til Christmas • Room in Your Heart • Scrooge • Thankful Heart • When Love Is Gone.
00312483...$16.99

Tim Burton's The Nightmare Before Christmas
This book features 11 songs from Tim Burton's creepy animated classic, with music and lyrics by Danny Elfman. Songs include: Jack's Lament • Jack's Obsession • Kidnap the Sandy Claws • Making Christmas • Oogie Boogie's Song • Poor Jack • Sally's Song • This Is Halloween • Town Meeting Song • What's This? • Finale/Reprise.
00312488...$16.99

A Sentimental Christmas Book
An outstanding collection of nearly 30 beloved Christmas favorites, including: All I Want for Christmas Is You • Blue Christmas • Christmas Lights • The Christmas Shoes • The Christmas Song (Chestnuts Roasting on an Open Fire) • Christmas Time Is Here • Christmases When You Were Mine • Fairytale of New York • Grown-Up Christmas List • Have Yourself a Merry Little Christmas • (There's No Place Like) Home for the Holidays • I'll Be Home for Christmas • Please Come Home for Christmas • Silver Bells • Somewhere in My Memory • Where Are You Christmas? • White Christmas • You're All I Want for Christmas • and more.
00236830...$14.99

Ultimate Christmas – 3rd Edition
100 seasonal favorites: Auld Lang Syne • Bring a Torch, Jeannette, Isabella • Carol of the Bells • The Chipmunk Song • Christmas Time Is Here • The First Noel • Frosty the Snow Man • Gesù Bambino • Happy Holiday • Happy Xmas (War Is Over) • Hymne • Jesu, Joy of Man's Desiring • Jingle-Bell Rock • March of the Toys • My Favorite Things • The Night Before Christmas Song • Pretty Paper • Silver and Gold • Silver Bells • Suzy Snowflake • What Child Is This • The Wonderful World of Christmas • and more.
00361399 ....$22.99

HAL•LEONARD®

Complete contents listings available online at www.halleonard.com
PRICES, CONTENTS, AND AVAILABILITY SUBJECT TO CHANGE WITHOUT NOTICE.

0419
302

HAL·LEONARD® HARMONICA PLAY-ALONG

Play your favorite songs quickly and easily!

Just follow the notation, listen to the audio to hear how the harmonica should sound, and then play along using the separate full-band backing tracks. The melody and lyrics are also included in the book in case you want to sing, or to simply help you follow along. The audio includes playback tools so you can adjust the recording to any tempo without changing pitch!

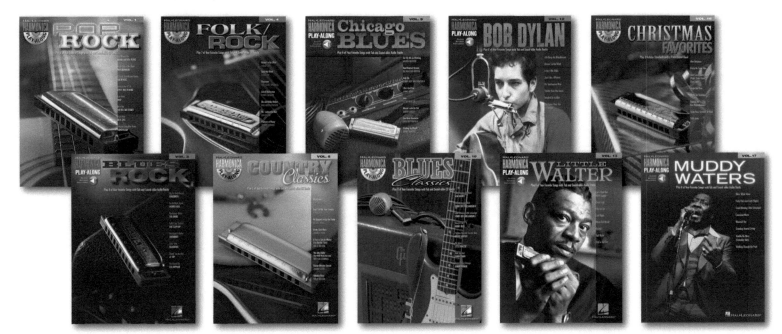

1. Pop/Rock
And When I Die • Bright Side of the Road • I Should Have Known Better • Low Rider • Miss You • Piano Man • Take the Long Way Home • You Don't Know How It Feels.
00000478 Book/CD Pack..........................$16.99

2. Rock Hits
Cowboy • Hand in My Pocket • Karma Chameleon • Middle of the Road • Run Around • Smokin' in the Boys Room • Train in Vain • What I like About You.
00000479 Book/CD Pack......................... $14.99

3. Blues/Rock
Big Ten Inch Record • On the Road Again • Road-house Blues • Rollin' and Tumblin' • Train Kept A-Rollin' • Train, Train • Waitin' for the Bus • You Shook Me.
00000481 Book/Online Audio $15.99

4. Folk/Rock
Blowin' in the Wind • Catch the Wind • Daydream • Eve of Destruction • Me and Bobby McGee • Mr. Tambourine Man • Pastures of Plenty.
00000482 Book/CD Pack......................... $14.99

5. Country Classics
Blue Bayou • Don't Tell Me Your Troubles • He Stopped Loving Her Today • Honky Tonk Blues • If You've Got the Money (I've Got the Time) • The Only Daddy That Will Walk the Line • Orange Blossom Special • Whiskey River.
00001004 Book/CD Pack......................... $14.99

6. Country Hits
Ain't Goin' down ('Til the Sun Comes Up) • Drive (For Daddy Gene) • Getcha Some • Here's a Quarter (Call Someone Who Cares) • Honkytonk U • One More Last Chance • Put Yourself in My Shoes • Turn It Loose.
00001013 Book/CD Pack $14.99

8. Pop Classics
Bluesette • Cherry Pink and Apple Blossom White • From Me to You • Love Me Do • Midnight Cowboy • Moon River • Peg O' My Heart • A Rainy Night in Georgia.
00001090 Book/Online Audio............... $14.99

9. Chicago Blues
Blues with a Feeling • Easy • Got My Mo Jo Working • Help Me • I Ain't Got You • Juke • Messin' with the Kid.
00001091 Book/Online Audio..................$15.99

10. Blues Classics
Baby, Scratch My Back • Eyesight to the Blind • Good Morning Little Schoolgirl • Honest I Do • I'm Your Hoochie Coochie Man • My Babe • Ride and Roll • Sweet Home Chicago.
00001093 Book/CD Pack $15.99

11. Christmas Carols
Angels We Have Heard on High • Away in a Manger • Deck the Hall • The First Noel • Go, Tell It on the Mountain • Jingle Bells • Joy to the World • O Little Town of Bethlehem.
00001296 Book/CD Pack..........................$12.99

12. Bob Dylan
All Along the Watchtower • Blowin' in the Wind • It Ain't Me Babe • Just like a Woman • Mr. Tambourine Man • Shelter from the Storm • Tangled up in Blue • The Times They Are A-Changin'.
00001326 Book/Online Audio..................$16.99

13. Little Walter
Can't Hold Out Much Longer • Crazy Legs • I Got to Go • Last Night • Mean Old World • Rocker • Sad Hours • You're So Fine.
00001334 Book/Online Audio $14.99

14. Jazz Standards
Autumn Leaves • Georgia on My Mind • Lullaby of Birdland • Meditation (Meditacao) • My Funny Valentine • Satin Doll • Some Day My Prince Will Come • What a Wonderful World.
00001335 Book/CD Pack..........................$16.99

15. Jazz Classics
All Blues • Au Privave • Comin' Home Baby • Song for My Father • Sugar • Sunny • Take Five • Work Song.
00001336 Book/CD Pack.......................... $14.99

16. Christmas Favorites
Blue Christmas • Frosty the Snow Man • Here Comes Santa Claus (Right down Santa Claus Lane) • Jingle-Bell Rock • Nuttin' for Christmas • Rudolph the Red-Nosed Reindeer • Santa Claus Is Comin' to Town • Silver Bells.
00001350 Book/CD Pack $14.99

17. Muddy Waters
Blow, Wind, Blow • Forty Days and Forty Nights • Good Morning Little Schoolgirl • Louisiana Blues • Mannish Boy • Standing Around Crying • Trouble No More (Someday Baby) • Walking Through the Park.
00821043 Book/Online Audio................. $14.99

HAL·LEONARD®
Order online from your favorite music retailer
at **www.halleonard.com**

Prices, content, and availability subject to change without notice.

0820
432

FastTrack is the fastest way for beginners to learn to play the instrument they just bought. **FastTrack** is different from other method books: we've made our book/audio packs user-friendly with plenty of cool songs that make it easy and fun for players to teach themselves. Plus, the last section of the books have the same songs so that students can form a band and jam together. Songbooks for guitar, bass, keyboard and drums are all compatible, and feature eight songs. All packs include great play-along audio with a professional-sounding back-up band.

FastTrack Bass
by Blake Neely & Jeff Schroedl

Level 1

00264732	Method Book/Online Media	$14.99
00697284	Method Book/Online Audio	$7.99
00696404	Method Book/Online Audio + DVD	$14.99
00697289	Songbook 1/Online Audio	$12.99
00695368	Songbook 2/Online Audio	$12.99
00696440	Rock Songbook with CD	$12.99
00696058	DVD	$7.99

Level 2

00697294	Method Book/Online Audio	$9.99
00697298	Songbook 1/Online Audio	$12.99
00695369	Songbook 2/Online Audio	$12.99

FastTrack Drum
by Blake Neely & Rick Mattingly

Level 1

00264733	Method Book/Online Media	$14.99
00697285	Method Book/Online Audio	$7.99
00696405	Method Book/Online Audio + DVD	$14.99
00697290	Songbook 1/Online Audio	$12.99
00695367	Songbook 2/Online Audio	$12.99
00696441	Rock Songbook with CD	$12.99
00696059	DVD	$7.99

Level 2

00697295	Method Book/Online Audio	$9.99
00697299	Songbook 1/Online Audio	$12.99
00695371	Songbook 2/Online Audio	$12.99

FastTrack Guitar
For Electric or Acoustic Guitar, or Both
by Blake Neely & Jeff Schroedl

Level 1

00264731	Method Book/Online Media	$14.99
00697282	Method Book/Online Audio	$7.99
00696403	Method Book/Online Audio + DVD	$14.99
00697287	Songbook 1/Online Audio	$12.99
00695343	Songbook 2/Online Audio	$12.99
00696438	Rock Songbook with CD	$12.99
00696057	DVD	$7.99

Level 2

00697286	Method Book/Online Audio	$9.99
00697296	Songbook/Online Audio	$14.99

Chords & Scales

00697291	Book/Online Audio	$10.99

FastTrack Keyboard
For Electric Keyboard, Synthesizer or Piano
by Blake Neely & Gary Meisner

Level 1

00264734	Method Book/Online Media	$14.99
00697283	Method Book/Online Audio	$7.99
00696406	Method Book/Online Audio + DVD	$14.99
00697288	Songbook 1/Online Audio	$12.99
00696439	Rock Songbook with CD	$12.99
00696060	DVD	$7.99

Level 2

00697293	Method Book/Online Audio	$9.99

Chords & Scales

00697292	Book/Online Audio	$9.99

FastTrack Harmonica
by Blake Neely & Doug Downing

Level 1

00695407	Method Book/Online Audio	$7.99
00695958	Mini Method Book with CD	$7.95
00820016	Mini Method/CD + Harmonica	$12.99
00695574	Songbook/Online Audio	$12.99

Level 2

00695889	Method Book/Online Audio	$9.99
00695891	Songbook with CD	$12.99

FastTrack Lead Singer
by Blake Neely

Level 1

00695408	Method Book/Online Audio	$7.99
00695410	Songbook/Online Audio	$14.99

Level 2

00695890	Method Book/Online Audio	$9.95
00695892	Songbook with CD	$12.95

FastTrack Saxophone
by Blake Neely

Level 1

00695241	Method Book/Online Audio	$7.99
00695409	Songbook/Online Audio	$14.99

FastTrack Ukulele
by Chad Johnson

Level 1

00114417	Method Book/Online Audio	$7.99
00158671	Songbook/Online Audio	$12.99

Level 2

00275508	Method Book/Online Audio	$9.99

FastTrack Violin
by Patrick Clark

Level 1

00141262	Method Book/Online Audio	$7.99

Visit Hal Leonard online at **www.halleonard.com**

0920
021